A
Prayer
That Moves
Heaven

Comfort and Hope
for Life's Most
Difficult Moments

Ron Mehl

Multnomah®Publishers *Sisters, Oregon*

A PRAYER THAT MOVES HEAVEN
published by Multnomah Publishers, Inc.
© 2002 by Ronald D. Mehl, Trustee

International Standard Book Number: 1-57673-885-X

Cover image by Photonica/Ryuichi Sato

Unless otherwise indicated, Scripture quotations are from:
The Holy Bible, New King James Version © 1984 by Thomas Nelson, Inc.

All other Scripture quotations are from:
The Holy Bible, King James Version (KJV)

New American Standard Bible ® (NASB)© 1960, 1977, 1995 by the Lockman
Foundation. Used by permission.

The Holy Bible, New International Version (NIV)© 1973, 1984 by International
Bible Society, used by permission of Zondervan Publishing House

Holy Bible, New Living Translation (NLT)© 1996. Used by permission of Tyndale
House Publishers, Inc. All rights reserved.

The Living Bible (TLB)© 1971. Used by permission of Tyndale House Publishers,
Inc. All rights reserved.

Multnomah is a trademark of Multnomah Publishers, Inc., and is registered in the
U.S. Patent and Trademark Office.
The colophon is a trademark of Multnomah Publishers, Inc.

Printed in the United States of America

For information:
MULTNOMAH PUBLISHERS, INC.•POST OFFICE BOX 1720•SISTERS, OREGON 97759
                    Library of Congress Cataloging-in-Publication Data

Mehl, Ron.
    A prayer that moves heaven : comfort and hope for life's most difficult moments /
by Ron Mehl.   p.cm.   ISBN 1-57673-885-X
    1. Bible. O.T. Chronicles, 2nd, XX, 1–30--Criticism, interpretation, etc. I. Title.
    BS1345 .2 .M44 2002   222' .64' 06--dc21   2001005805

                    02 03 04 05 06—10 9 8 7 6 5 4 3 2 1 0

Dedicated with love and affection
to
Warner Kingsley Mehl,

our second grandchild.
I pray that he will, by his prayers,
move the heart of God.

TABLE OF CONTENTS

ACKNOWLEDGMENTS

In my lifetime I have never seen a day in which the world seems so troubled and yet for many as if there are so few answers. But the truth is that there is an answer. In difficult times God wants to move. As you read through these pages, you'll discover that God is looking for people through whom He can move. Whenever God encounters praying people, He is always moved.

This book was born out of my personal experience with God and His Word. God has said, "If you'll call unto Me, I will show you great and mighty things which thou knowest not." I've always believed that you can't have a movement of God without a man or woman being moved by God. That's what I hope you'll see in this book. I believe with you that God might move and that He'll move through us.

There could never be enough kind words said about Multnomah Publishers and its president, Don Jacobson. Don and his gifted and caring staff have always meant the world to me. I so appreciate their partnership. They've blessed me greatly.

I want to especially thank my close friend Larry Libby, whom I declare here and now as undebatably the greatest editor of all. What a treasure Larry has been to me. Larry, thank you for making me look so much better than I deserve.

Also, a kind word is due to the people I serve with. From the congregation to the staff…I am very privileged. They are the best, and they have made my life such a joy.

Finally, I have been and am continually moved by the family that God has given me. My wife, Joyce; our two sons, Ron Jr. and Mark, along with their sweet wives, Elizabeth and Stephanie; and, of course, the family treasures—our two grandchildren, Liesl and Warner Mehl. I love them and bless them for being such a joy to me.

It happened after this that the people of Moab with the people of Ammon, and others with them besides the Ammonites, came to battle against Jehoshaphat. Then some came and told Jehoshaphat, saying, "A great multitude is coming against you from beyond the sea, from Syria; and they are in Hazazon Tamar" (which is En Gedi). And Jehoshaphat feared, and set himself to seek the LORD, and proclaimed a fast throughout all Judah. So Judah gathered together to ask help from the LORD; and from all the cities of Judah they came to seek the LORD.

Then Jehoshaphat stood in the assembly of Judah and Jerusalem, in the house of the LORD, before the new court, and said: "O LORD God of our fathers, are You not God in heaven, and do You not rule over all the kingdoms of the nations, and in Your hand is there not power and might, so that no one is able to withstand You? Are You not our God, who drove out the inhabitants of this land before Your people Israel, and gave it to the descendants of Abraham Your friend forever? And they dwell in it, and have built You a sanctuary in it for Your name, saying, 'If disaster comes upon us—sword, judgment, pestilence, or famine—we will stand before this temple and in Your presence (for Your name is in this temple), and cry out to You in our affliction, and You will hear and save.' And *now, here are the people of Ammon, Moab, and Mount Seir—whom You would not let Israel invade when they came out of the land of Egypt, but they turned from them and did not destroy them—here they are, rewarding us by coming to throw us out of Your possession which You have given us to inherit. O our God, will You not judge them? For we have no power against this great multitude that is coming against us; nor do we know what to do, but our eyes are upon You." Now all Judah, with their little ones, their wives, and their children, stood before the LORD.*

Then the Spirit of the LORD came upon Jahaziel the son of Zechariah, the son of Benaiah, the son of Jeiel, the son of Mattaniah, a Levite of the sons of Asaph, in the midst of the assembly. And he said, "Listen, all you of Judah and you inhabitants of Jerusalem, and you, King Jehoshaphat! Thus says the LORD to you: 'Do not be afraid nor dismayed because of this great multitude, for the battle is not yours, but God's. Tomorrow go down against them. They will surely come up by the Ascent of Ziz, and you will find them at the end of the brook before the Wilderness of Jeruel. You will not need to fight in this bat-tle. Position yourselves, stand still and see the salvation of the LORD, who is with you, O Judah and Jerusalem!' Do not fear or be dismayed; tomorrow go out against them, for the LORD is with you." And Jehoshaphat bowed his head with his face to the ground, and all Judah and the

*inhabitants of Jerusalem bowed before the LORD, worship-
ing the LORD. Then the Levites of the children of the
Kohathites and of the children of the Korahites stood up to
praise the LORD God of Israel with voices loud and high.*

*So they rose early in the morning and went out into
the Wilderness of Tekoa; and as they went out,
Jehoshaphat stood and said, "Hear me, O Judah and you
inhabitants of Jerusalem: Believe in the LORD your God,
and you shall be established; believe His prophets, and you
shall prosper." And when he had consulted with the people,
he appointed those who should sing to the LORD, and who
should praise the beauty of holiness, as they went out
before the army and were saying:*

"Praise the LORD, for His mercy endures forever."

*Now when they began to sing and to praise, the LORD
set ambushes against the people of Ammon, Moab, and
Mount Seir, who had come against Judah; and they were
defeated. For the people of Ammon and Moab stood up
against the inhabitants of Mount Seir to utterly kill and
destroy them. And when they had made an end of the
inhabitants of Seir, they helped to destroy one another.*

*So when Judah came to a place overlooking the
wilderness, they looked toward the multitude; and there
were their dead bodies, fallen on the earth. No one had
escaped. When Jehoshaphat and his people came to take
away their spoil, they found among them an abundance*

of valuables on the dead bodies, and precious jewelry, which they stripped off for themselves, more than they could carry away; and they were three days gathering the spoil because there was so much. And on the fourth day they assembled in the Valley of Berachah, for there they blessed the LORD; therefore the name of that place was called The Valley of Berachah until this day. Then they returned, every man of Judah and Jerusalem, with Jehoshaphat in front of them, to go back to Jerusalem with joy, for the LORD had made them rejoice over their enemies. So they came to Jerusalem, with stringed instruments and harps and trumpets, to the house of the LORD. And the fear of God was on all the kingdoms of those countries when they heard that the LORD had fought against the enemies of Israel. Then the realm of Jehoshaphat was quiet, for his God gave him rest all around.

2 CHRONICLES 20:1–30

1

Just an Ordinary Day

*Then some came and told Jehoshaphat, saying,
"A great multitude is coming against you
from beyond the sea...."*

2 CHRONICLES 20:2

When Jehoshaphat got up that morning, there was nothing in his appointment book about a life-defining crisis. Efficient as his aides and secretaries may have been, there was no mention of the event that would mark his life forever.

Can you visualize that day, the day Jehoshaphat would remember for the rest of his life?

Dawn came bright and clear. He got out of his bed, stretched, and shuffled into his morning routine. After he had washed and dressed, it was time for his morning prayers. He probably knelt before an open window just as Daniel would do centuries later. It's easy to imagine him praying something like this:

Sovereign Lord, God of my great-great-great-grandfather David, I belong to You. I look to You on this new dawn for strength, wisdom, and grace to lead Your covenant people. I depend on You, Almighty One. Keep me from relaxing my vigilance, as my great-great-grandfather Solomon relaxed his vigilance to His own hurt and to the hurt of Your people. Keep me from presumption, as my grandfather Rehoboham presumed against You, to the sundering of the nation. Keep me from pride, as my father Asa was too proud to seek You in his illness, and he died. Ah, Sovereign Lord, as my day unrolls like a scroll, little by little, moment by moment, grant Your servant discernment to make those decisions that please You and bless Your people, the sheep of Your pasture. Amen.

An aide stepped discreetly into the room as the king rose from his knees. In a quiet voice the trusted servant delivered the morning news—what little there was of it. Nothing untoward had happened in the night. No messengers had arrived bearing tidings—either good or ill. Jerusalem had been quiet, apart from a few minor domestic spats and a runaway donkey or two.

As Jehoshaphat nibbled at his figs and pomegranate, the aide briefed him on the latest reports and corre-

spondence from foreign leaders, from Judah's ambassadors, from his hand-picked judges in the cities, and from his captains in the field. The army's idol eradication unit continued on pace, destroying all vestiges of idolatry and the shrines at the high places across the land. The king's overnight trip to Beth Shemesh was still on track: Security was in place, and the judge of the city and the army commander on the Philistine frontier were looking forward to the meetings.

It was just an ordinary day.

Or was it?

I n fact, there was nothing ordinary at all about that day. Before the sun had advanced across the blue Jerusalem sky, Jehoshaphat would find himself trying to absorb the most shocking, fearful news a king can receive.

How would he respond? How would *you* respond?

PRINCIPLE #I:
Walk ready every day…
you never know when the Edomites are coming.

I remember an ordinary day in my own life, a number of years ago now. I was in my office pursuing all those normal routines I've done thousands of times in my years of ministry. I felt well and strong, but then, I'd always felt well and strong. Blessed with an athletic body and an iron constitution, I hardly knew what it was to be sick.

A complete physical just a few days before had confirmed that obvious fact once again. I was fit and healthy. Why, then, was my secretary telling me that my doctor was on the phone?

"It's about one of your blood tests, Ron," he told me. "I've got some concerns I'd like to discuss with you. Can you come in...right away?"

Now that was strange. What was this all about? I told my secretary I had to be out for a couple of hours and headed out the door. I already had plans to meet my wife, Joyce, and to join another couple for lunch at the mall.

The doctor invited me into his office and had me sit down. I wasn't liking the way this meeting seemed to be shaping up. I wasn't liking the look on his face.

"Ron," he said, "the news isn't good. You have leukemia."

He began to explain this cancer of the blood to me, but it really wasn't necessary. A pastor friend of mine in Minneapolis had just died of the disease. I knew about leukemia; I just couldn't believe I had it.

I met Joyce outside the mall and briefly told her the news. We didn't even have time to absorb the shock or talk about it before we met our friends. What an odd lunch that turned out to be! We sat with our friends and talked about all those trivial, lighthearted things you'd expect friends to gab about over lunch, yet it was as though Joyce and I were on automatic pilot. We said the expected things and smiled at the expected times, but a dense, numbing fog had settled over everything. Somehow, the conversation seemed to be coming from far away.

Leukemia!

Just that quickly, *everything* changed. All of our plans, dreams, and expectations were suddenly put on hold. Would I be able to continue in the ministry? Would I live out the year? Would I see my boys graduate from high school? Would I see my own grandchildren? Was my life insurance adequate? A thousand questions coursed through my mind, and answers were hard to find.

"A great multitude is coming against you from beyond the sea, from Syria; and they are in Hazazon Tamar."

More times than I can number over the last twenty-eight years, I have had the opportunity to stand beside someone in our large Beaverton flock who has received crushing, unexpected news. I've seen every reaction you could possibly imagine—rage, despair, weeping, terror, and stunned silence.

"A great multitude is coming against you."

I've also seen those who experience the emotions of fear or grief but turn almost immediately to the Lord.

That's what King Jehoshaphat did on that ordinary day when the clear blue sky suddenly buckled and fell in upon him. That's what Ron and Joyce Mehl did, too, when the earth lurched beneath our feet and every thought of normal life went out the window, never to return.

Walking in Grace and Mercy

And Jehoshaphat feared, and set himself to seek the LORD.

2 CHRONICLES 20:3

Y ou and I are creatures of time. Even the wisest, brightest, and most perceptive among us cannot see beyond the present moment. For all of the technical brilliance of our scientists and inventors, no one has found a way to peer even two seconds into the future. As James wrote, "Why, you do not even know what will happen tomorrow. What is your life? You are a mist that appears for a little while and then vanishes" (James 4:14, NIV).

When we open our eyes each morning, we have no idea what the next twenty-four hours will bring. When I was in Bible college, I remember a professor with a reputation for suddenly springing pop quizzes on the class. Those things were murder. You didn't have the option of waiting until two or three days before the big midterm and final exams to cram your head full of facts. You knew that on any given day, you might walk into his class and find yourself staring at a quiz, testing your knowledge of every reading in the textbook and everything he'd covered in class up to that point.

How unfair can you get? You had to study *every night* for this guy's class. You had to take notes every day, read the assignments every day, and review the material every day, or you might find yourself caught short in the moment of testing.

Jehoshaphat found himself staring at the biggest test of his life, and he had no time to cram, review his notes, speed-read the text, or collect his thoughts.

The enemy was on his doorstep.

Jehoshaphat's great-great-grandfather, Solomon, once wrote: "If you faint in the day of adversity, your strength is small" (Proverbs 24:10). But when is that day of adversity? When will it come? Will there be any warning? Any premonition? King Jehoshaphat had no advance notice, and when trouble crashed into his life, he was gripped with fear. It shook him to the core. It must have felt like a punch in the stomach.

He staggered. He groaned. But he didn't faint.

Instead, he turned instantly to the God of his fathers and poured out his heart.

What kept Jehoshaphat from fainting in the day of testing? What kept him from flying into a blind terror or tumbling into a bottomless despair? How was he able to turn to the Lord the way he did and trust God with this fearful news?

Jehoshaphat's secret was simple. When it came time to run for the Lord's help, he didn't have very far to go. In fact, he walked with God every day. When the messenger burst into the king's court with his dire news, Jehoshaphat didn't have to scramble around looking for the Lord's phone number: *Now, where did I leave that thing? Was it in my old address book? Didn't I keep it on a note in the top drawer? Didn't I see it on a sticky note on the fridge?*

The Lord and Jehoshaphat had probably already

PRINCIPLE #2:
Set your heart's direction every morning…
make up your mind to follow Him.

---

been in conversation that day—perhaps that very hour. It was completely natural for the king to turn to God in this moment of fear and distress. Imagine yourself walking with Jesus Christ along the road. Suddenly a lion leaps out of the brush and confronts you. What do you do? You instinctively grasp the Lord's arm and cry out, "Jesus, help me!"

You don't have to make an appointment to see a counselor, and you don't have to check out a book on fear management from the library, because Jesus Himself is right beside you, and you've been conversing with Him all morning long. The more you remain in conversation with the Lord throughout the day, the more "available" you will find Him when you run headlong into a trial. The more you study and read and meditate on His Word, the closer those words will be to your heart when you fall into crisis.

How do we know that Jehoshaphat walked with God? The evidence is right there in Scripture. Second Chronicles 17 tells us that "the LORD was with Jehoshaphat, because he walked in the former ways of his [great-great-great-grandfather] David; he did not seek the Baals, but sought the God of his father, and walked in His commandments" (vv. 3–4).

The king had certainly made a terrible error in judgment when he allied himself—both militarily and maritally—with the evil king Ahab of Israel. Yet even when he was in battle at Ahab's side, and the enemies' chariot captains surrounded him, "Jehoshaphat cried out, and the LORD helped him" (2 Chronicles 18:31).

Upon his return to Jerusalem, the king felt the sting of the Lord's rebuke for that foolish decision, and his family would reap terrible consequences in the years to come. Nevertheless, the prophet Jehu told him, "good things are found in you, in that you have removed the wooden images from the land, and have prepared your heart to seek God" (2 Chronicles 19:3).

The New International Version renders that last verse, *"You...have set your heart on seeking God."* Those who set their hearts on seeking God every day don't have to look up His address in the day of trouble. Those who cultivate the presence of God as a daily habit of life don't have to start from scratch when they need Him the most.

The Bible says, "Seek the LORD and His strength; Seek His face *continually"* (Psalm 105:4, NASB, italics mine). In other words, we're to go looking for the Lord's strength every day and every hour of the day— not just when we find ourselves in trouble or danger. His strength is always there, of course, and ever available to His children. But if we've allowed clutter to build up in our relationship with God, if we've allowed that living, pulsing sense of His reality in our lives to fade, our faith may be very small at just the time when we need faith the most.

A friend once told me about a small boy in Oklahoma named Billy, who had Down's syndrome. One day Billy visited a little church in town with the pastor's son, who had befriended him. When the pastor said, "Is there anyone here who wants to give his or her life to Jesus?" Billy immediately lifted his hand.

From that time on, Billy came every Sunday, choosing pew number two as his designated spot. And if you happened to get there first and sit down in that pew, he'd sit right in your lap.

Sometimes, during worship, God would move on Billy's heart, and he would lift his hands, tears filling his eyes and spilling down his cheeks. Five minutes or so later, God would move on others in the congregation. It always seemed that when God began to touch people's hearts in that little church, Billy was the first one to sense His presence. Others would follow after.

After telling me that story, my friend speculated that Billy didn't have a lot of clutter in his life. When the Holy Spirit began to touch people, Billy was wide open; nothing hindered his response.

Why is it so difficult for us to hear from God sometimes? Because our lives are so often cluttered with cares and worries and preoccupations and noise that God can't get through to us. But Billy was a simple young man, and the Lord had immediate access to his heart.

In the book of Hebrews we find this strong invitation:

> Let us therefore come boldly to the throne of grace, that we may obtain mercy and find grace to help in time of need. (Hebrews 4:16)

I think there are a couple of ways to look at this verse. Yes, I can certainly run to the throne of grace when I'm in trouble and it's a time of need. But in an ever deeper sense I hear this verse saying, "Why don't you walk and talk with God every day and store up some grace and mercy? Then, in the time of your great trouble and fear, you will already know and be experiencing the grip of His strong hand."

PRINCIPLE #3:
Drink deeply every day...
from His fountain of mercy and grace.

Life is unpredictable. Challenges are unavoidable. I see this verse urging us to come boldly again and again to the throne of grace, keeping our mercy-and-grace tank full, *because we never know when we will desperately need it.*

I'll let you in on a little secret. The older I get, the more I just want to *live* at His throne of grace and mercy. I want to pitch my tent and set up camp right there. I want to spend my life in that place. I may be preaching or counseling or writing or spending time with my family, but I want to keep at least one foot—one part of my heart and soul—before that throne where the grace flows. I want to live with a deep, abiding confidence in God, because I know Him and He knows me, and I'm no stranger to His courts. I want to be able to look the enemy in the eye and say, "I know who and what I am dealing with, and I know my God is greater than anything you can throw at me. I've been to the throne of grace before, and I am well acquainted with His mercy and power."

I've learned that confidence in God always brings courage before our enemy.

3

Truths about Testing

It happened after this…

2 CHRONICLES 20:1

Whe I think of Jehoshaphat's cry for mercy on that anything-but-ordinary day, I'm reminded of three principles that weave their way through the pages of the Bible.

1. *You can plan on tests from God.*

In his book *The Road Less Traveled*, M. Scott Peck makes this point: "Once we truly know that life is difficult—once we truly understand and accept it—then life is no longer difficult."[1] It's the same with the Christian life. Scripture assures us over and over again that we will experience trials and testings in our lives—difficult circumstances allowed by the hand of our Father.

In John 16:33, Jesus told His disciples, "In the world you will have tribulation; but be of good cheer, I have overcome the world." David assured us that "a righteous man may have many troubles, but the LORD delivers him from them all" (Psalm 34:19, NIV). Passages like Romans 5:3 and James 1:2 just assume that trials will be part of our lives—and teach us how to respond.

Once you know and accept the fact that hard times and difficult situations are part and parcel of the Christian life—that they are neither strange nor out of place nor unusual—then the way ahead becomes easier. *Of course* I will have trials in my life. *Of course* I will experience testing and difficulty, along with the rest of humanity. But if my Father has allowed that trial to touch my life, then He's going to show me what to do, and He will be there with me all along the way. He will deliver me in and through my pressures and heartaches.

2. *You need to prepare your heart NOW for those inevitable tests.*

Jehoshaphat had prepared his heart to seek God (2 Chronicles 19:3). That word *prepare* can also mean *to fix* or *fasten.* Scripture also says the king's heart "took delight in the ways of the LORD" (2 Chronicles 17:6).

Nobody can be completely ready for devastating

news. When you hear that a vast army is marching toward you, when you hear that you have a killer disease in your bloodstream, when you hear that your best friend's plane is missing, you're going to be staggered by that news. Yet if your heart is fixed and fastened on the faithfulness of God, and if you are daily delighting in His presence, His Spirit, and His Word, those tests will not crush you. You will be able to turn immediately to God for help…and find it!

3. *When the tests do come, focus on God's promises.*

In this account, that's exactly what happened. Jehoshaphat didn't weep and wail before the Lord, he zeroed in immediately on the promises of God's Word. Faith doesn't demand explanations from God, but rests on His promises.

When I meet with people who are in crisis, I often suggest that they do three things: *get alone, get a promise,* and *get serious.* In other words, base your prayers for deliverance and help on the unchanging Word of God. Get a grip on God and His promises and don't look back or let go.

Second Chronicles 20 begins with the words *It happened after this….*

And every good Bible student asks the question "After *what?*"

After several things, and most of them good. Jehoshaphat's life had been spared when he foolishly went to war at the side of evil King Ahab. After a close brush with death and a stern rebuke from the prophet Jehu, Jehoshaphat got serious about his walk with God, and he resolved to seek the Lord with all his heart. He appointed godly men as judges throughout the land, and he sought to turn the hearts of the people back toward the God of David.

And after all these noble efforts, after all these good works, after this positive, commendable start...the roof fell in! That's the pattern so many times in Scripture. After great blessing comes great testing.

After Joshua and the army of Israel experienced an overwhelming victory at Jericho, they fell flat on their faces and suffered humiliating casualties at a little backwater town called Ai.

It happened with Jesus, too, after being baptized in the Jordan. The sky had opened, the Holy Spirit had descended upon Him, and the Father had declared His love for Him in mighty words that thundered across the landscape.

And then...did He have time to savor those words?

Did He get a few golden weeks to enjoy that new phase of life? No. The Father's words had hardly ceased echoing across the Jordan valley before "the Spirit drove Him into the wilderness. And He was there in the wilderness forty days, tempted by Satan" (Mark 1:12–13).

The disciples had just experienced the elation of participating in a stunning miracle: feeding five thousand men from one boy's little lunch. They had heard the crowd shout, "This is truly the Prophet who is to come into the world" (John 6:14). It must have been a crowning, exultant moment for these men who had left everything to follow the Teacher from Galilee.

Yet just a few hours later they found themselves rowing for their lives in a storm, in the sea, in the night—and where was Jesus?

I've come to believe that Satan's radar detects the blessings of God in the lives of His children. And just when that believer begins to feel secure and confident, he moves in to test and try that man or woman, hoping to catch one of God's kids unawares.

If you have experienced a season of effective ministry, peace of heart, and multiple blessings, thank God! Rejoice in those good things. You can say with the apostle Paul, "I know what it is to be in need, and I know what it is to have plenty" (Philippians 4:12, NIV).

But understand that a period of challenge and testing may drop into your life at any moment. Be ready!

1. M. Scott Peck, The Road Less Traveled (New York: Touchstone, 1980), 15.

4

The Facts...or the TRUTH?

"O LORD God of our fathers, are You not God in heaven, and do You not rule over all the kingdoms of the nations, and in Your hand is there not power and might, so that no one is able to withstand You?"

2 CHRONICLES 20:6

Jehoshaphat had no reason to doubt his messengers. There is no record that he wasted time in foolish denial. *"Wait a minute. Are you guys dead sure you saw an actual invasion force? C'mon! Really? You were close enough to see for sure that they were soldiers? Could you see weapons? Armor? Are you sure about that 'great multitude' business? The light and shadows can play tricks on a fella's eyes sometimes. Maybe it was just some kind of caravan heading up toward Syria. Maybe it was a migrating herd of deer."*

Jehoshaphat immediately accepted the facts as they were placed before him—terrible as they were. He understood and admitted that a vast army of hostile, allied powers had swept in from the east, had made the turn around the southern end of the Dead Sea, and were even now marching north toward Jerusalem.

He acknowledged the facts. But he also knew that facts aren't everything.

What are the facts for people at times?

The fact is, your marriage is in very serious trouble.
The fact is, you're heading toward bankruptcy.
The fact is, your ministry is going nowhere.
The fact is, you've got a grave health problem, and the doctors aren't holding out much hope.
The fact is, your kids have turned their backs on what you've taught them, and have drifted far from the Lord.
The fact is, your unemployment is about to run out, and you can't find work anywhere.

Yes, there are certainly difficult and challenging facts you and I need to deal with every day of our lives. But there is also the *truth*. And if you don't take God into account, you may have the facts, but you will not have the truth. That is why the Lord gave us His Word, so that we might stand on His promises in the face of over-whelming circumstances.

The facts may say that you are in great danger or that there is little hope for your life...your marriage...your children...your ministry. But the *truth* is that God says, "Nothing is impossible with Me." Just about any reasonable person can look around and see that there is a great problem or difficulty. But it takes another kind of person to really see God's truth, to see what God has promised.

Please remember this: *There are times in life when the facts do not line up with the truth.* What your eyes and ears and logic are screaming at you may not be the truth at all. In fact, if you have left God out of your deliberations, it is *not* the truth. The pages of Scripture are filled with men and women who faced the naked facts of their situation, then saw beyond the facts to an all-powerful, sovereign God who is greater than any situation or circumstance.

Jehoshaphat certainly had the data about the invading armies. He saw the desperate situation and was

---

PRINCIPLE #4:
Look beyond the facts...
until you see the Truth.

---

afraid. Of course he was! But before that fear could immobilize him, before that terror could turn his bones to Jell-O, he quickly filled his eyes with God and his mind with the promises of God's Word. The people who will experience miracles in their lives are those who look up from the hard realities of their circumstances and see the Lord.

I love the way the king approached God in his prayer; he began reciting the truth right back to the God of truth. In verse 6 of 2 Chronicles 20, he says:

> "O LORD God of our fathers, are You not God in heaven, and do You not rule over all the kingdoms of the nations, and in Your hand is there not power and might, so that no one is able to withstand You?"

In other words, *"Aren't You the God who rules over all things?"* Jehoshaphat reminds himself of who God is—that He is ruler and that He is sovereign and all-powerful. He is saying, "Lord, You're the one in charge. There is nothing too hard for You."

Old Testament prayers are mighty because they don't start with the problem or need. Instead, they begin by focusing on the character and attributes of our awesome God. These are promise-centered prayers rather than problem-centered prayers. Have you ever prayed that way in a life crisis? Have you ever spent the first five minutes of your prayer just rehearsing what you know about God—His love, His mercy, His tenderness, His wisdom, His sovereign power? I can tell you this: By the time you get around to mentioning your hurts and needs and fears, they won't seem quite so overwhelming.

In verse 7, Jehoshaphat went on to pray:

"Are you not our God, who drove out the inhabitants of this land before Your people Israel, and gave it to the descendants of Abraham Your friend forever?"

In other words, *"Aren't You the God who delivered us before?"* After you've reflected on the person and character of God, it's good to remember a little history. "Aren't You the very same God who knocked down the walls of Jericho? Aren't You the same Lord who stopped the sun and the moon in their courses so that Joshua's army could win the day against his enemies? Aren't You the same Almighty One who crushed the armies of Midian before Gideon and a little band of three hundred men?"

Don't forget just whom it is you're praying to!

Don't forget that your heavenly Father does not change like shifting shadows. Don't forget that Jesus Christ is the same yesterday, today, and forever. He has delivered people from terrible situations for thousands of years. Delivering people in great crisis is nothing new to God. You're not His first client!

In verse 9 the king reminded the Lord of the words Solomon had prayed at the dedication of the temple:

> "'If disaster comes upon us—sword, judgment, pestilence, or famine—we will stand before this temple and in Your presence (for Your name is in this temple), and cry out to You in our affliction, and You will hear and save.'"

In other words, *"Aren't You the God who responds to our cry?"* There is one prayer that always seems to get God's attention. It's the heart cry of His people. The most powerful kind of prayer has nothing to do with style, polish, technique, or a particular arrangement of impressive-sounding words. It's simply a child of God crying out to heaven. I know what it's like to feel so burdened that all I could do was cry out to God with deep groanings. But I'm not the first one who has poured out his heart to God—crying out in distress and fear and great need—and found Him faithful. Just

as a toddler's cry of distress gains the immediate attention of his mother, so men and women throughout
the pages of the Bible have cried out to their heavenly
Father. And He inclines His ear to their voice, moving
heaven and earth to meet their needs. Groaning and
crying out to God is a language He readily under-
stands (Romans 8:26–27).

In verse 12, the king begins to wrap up his prayer
with these words: "O our God, will You not judge
them?"

In other words, "Aren't You the God who wants to
move on behalf of Your people again, Lord? Don't You
want to deliver us again for the glory of Your great
name? Won't You show us that same mightiness You
showed to Your people of long ago?"

This is the kind of prayer that moves heaven—
where you remember who God is and what He has
done and invite this very same God, this God of power
and wonder and compassion, to step into your situation and make a difference in your life. It's not as
though God needs reminding about who He is or what
He has done; I'm reminding myself! I'm the one who
needs to remember. And in remembering, I will begin
to pray with faith and joy.

Finally, Jehoshaphat prayed:

"For we have no power against this great multitude that is coming against us; nor do we know what to do, but our eyes are upon You."

That's a humble prayer. It's the prayer of a man who is completely overwhelmed, overmatched, over his head...and willing to admit it. When you are hard pressed, when you are devastated by circumstances, whether it is leukemia, a failing marriage, unemployment, or trouble of any sort—remember Peter's words: "God resists the proud but gives grace to the humble" (1 Peter 5:5).

Being humble means realizing and acknowledging who we really are—and who God is. It is freely admitting our vast inadequacies before One who is thoroughly adequate to meet every need.

I think this is one of the reasons the Lord has been so gracious to me over the years. I've never been ashamed to let Him—or anybody else—know that I'm in way over my head. You see, I never have to worry about "blowing my cover" and having people find out that Ron Mehl is inadequate and out of his league. I tell them right up front! I let them know from the get-go that God really is my strength and my wisdom and my help. I tell everyone I can that unless the Lord intervenes for me, unless He empowers me and grants me discernment and perseverance and patience, I will fall flat on my face.

Jehoshaphat may very well have learned to cry out to God from his own daddy, King Asa. He would certainly have known the story of how Asa and the army of Judah found themselves facing Zerah the Ethiopian, with an army of a million men and three hundred chariots in the vanguard.

Asa knew how to count. He knew he was vastly outgunned and outnumbered. The simple facts said he was finished—and all of Judah with him. But the king cried out to a God who was bigger than the facts: "LORD, there is no one like you to help the powerless against the mighty. Help us, O LORD our God, for we rely on you, and in your name we have come against this vast army. O LORD, you are our God; do not let man prevail against you" (2 Chronicles 14:11, NIV).

What happened next could not be explained by any military strategist in the world. The Bible tells us that the vast Ethiopian army was "crushed before the LORD and his forces" (v. 13, NIV).

Looking back beyond his father, Asa, Jehoshaphat might also have been inspired by the biblical account of Abraham and Sarah.

Against all hope, Abraham in hope believed
and so became the father of many nations,
just as it had been said to him, "So shall
your offspring be." Without weakening in
his faith, he faced the fact that his body was
as good as dead—since he was about a hundred years old—and that Sarah's womb was
also dead. Yet he did not waver through
unbelief regarding the promise of God, but
was strengthened in his faith and gave glory
to God, being fully persuaded that God had
power to do what he had promised.
(Romans 4:18–21, NIV)

The facts? Well, they couldn't have been any clearer.
Abraham and Sarah were many years past childbearing
age. Abraham's body was "as good as dead," and
"Sarah's womb was also dead."

Those are called the facts of life, right?

Abraham faced those facts, and admitted their
accuracy. *But he knew that facts do not always equal
truth.* "Against all hope, Abraham in hope believed."
You don't have truth until you bring God into the
equation, and God had told Abraham that his descendants from his own body would be as numerous as the
stars of the heavens.

Abraham saw the facts but believed the truth.

If you look only at the facts, you will end up in hopelessness and despair. In the days of the old sailing ships, there was a phenomenon out at sea that sailors feared worse than a great gale with mountainous waves. What seamen feared most was a dead calm, where the wind died away for weeks at a time and ships were caught in the grip of powerful ocean currents. Often they found themselves going around and around in great circles, day after day, week after week.

There have been occasions when others have boarded ships becalmed in this way. In some cases they found ample supplies of food and water, but a crew that had died or gone mad in their hopelessness.

We live in a world like that today. There are people all around us who are going in circles, with no hope and no options. They go around and around in the same frustrations, the same fears, the same habits, the same sins, week after week, year after year. So many people know the facts but have never learned the truth.

We seek to teach our children "the facts" in school, but we carefully guard them from being exposed to the truth. We listen to our scientists and educators speak about the origin of life and the origin of the universe, and they cite this piece of data and that piece of data. But they give no place to the Designer of all the awesome majesty and beauty that surrounds us.

Science and education today are long on "facts" but tragically short on the truth. Unless they include an almighty and loving Creator in their equations and deliberations, they will be left with weak, tentative theories that don't really make sense or fit together.

Jehoshaphat considered the facts, but only in the context of truth.

And so should we.

5

What Do You See?

"O our God, will You not judge them?
For we have no power
against this great multitude that is coming against us."

2 CHRONICLES 20:12

W hen you are facing an impossible situation or a difficult, frightening experience, the first thing you have to ask is, What do I see?

The messenger told Jehoshaphat exactly what he was facing. He told him of the vast army of allied enemies and where he had last seen them. Jehoshaphat had certainly seen enemy armies and close combat before—in fact, he had probably been closer to the action than he ever wanted to be! In his mind's eye, he could picture it all: the dark mass of humanity, tens of thousands of grim-faced warriors marching through Hazazon Tamar.

That's a picture that could burn into your retinas

and not let you see anything else. But Jehoshaphat deliberately turned his eyes toward heaven. And when you see God and begin to pray, your perspective changes. You see things differently.

Thinking back on the stories of great heroes in the Bible, I always ask myself, *What did they see?* What did David, just a young teenager at the time, see when he stood against Goliath? Did he see a nine-foot, blaspheming monster in armor plating...*or did he see a huge God, who made Goliath seem vertically challenged?*

What did Daniel see when he was thrown into the lion's den? Did he see ravenous, man-eating lions...*or did he have a vast vision of his God that made the lions look like tabby cats?*

Obviously, David and Daniel and Jehoshaphat saw the enemy. But they also saw God. In order for God to do something, it is essential that you see both.

The fact is, when you see God, everything else seems smaller. The situation you face seems less intimidating and overwhelming. The odds against you don't seem to matter so much. If you focus on God, the obstacles will always shrink because of your changed perspective. Our problems and our trials may seem huge to us—mountainous, towering, overwhelming—but they are insignificant to the mighty God of the universe.

Jeremiah came to the same conclusion. Looking up into heaven, the embattled prophet exclaimed, "Ah, Lord GOD! Behold, You have made the heavens and the earth by Your great power and outstretched arm. There is nothing too hard for You" (Jeremiah 32:17).

I can't help but think of Elisha and his servant, who were staying in the city of Dothan. One morning the servant took a little walk outside—and got the surprise of his life.

So one night the king of Syria sent a great army with many chariots and horses to surround the city. When the prophet's servant got up early the next morning and went outside, there were troops, horses, and chariots everywhere.

"Alas, my master, what shall we do now?" he cried out to Elisha.

"Don't be afraid!" Elisha told him. "For our army is bigger than theirs!"

Then Elisha prayed, "Lord, open his eyes and let him see!" And the Lord opened the young man's eyes so that he could see horses of fire and chariots of fire everywhere upon the mountain! (2 Kings 6:14–17, TLB)

The facts were indisputable. Elisha and Gehazai were completely surrounded. By almost anybody's scorecard, that meant the game was up. That they were finished. Those were the simple facts. Anybody with two eyes in his head could have seen that. There was no way out of that city because the Syrian army had completely encircled it. All right, *but who was encircling the Syrian army?* Gehazai had the data, but he didn't have the truth. Not until Elisha prayed for him, "Lord, open his eyes!" Then he could see. Then he knew the truth.

Our prayer should always be, "Lord, here are the facts as best as I can see. But I know that my vision is poor and dim and sometimes I don't see very far at all. Lord, open my eyes to the truth—to the truth that is everywhere upon the mountains surrounding the facts."

PRINCIPLE #5:
Welcome your fear…
as long as it drives you to your knees.

What, then, do you do with your fear when you find yourself facing dark and trying circumstances?

There is nothing wrong with being afraid. Who *wouldn't* have been afraid of such news? The king would have been foolish not to fear a vast, invading army sweeping toward Jerusalem like a flash flood. And it wasn't as though Jehoshaphat feared for his own skin alone; he was shepherd to hundreds of thousands of men, women, and little ones. Every eye in the kingdom looked to their king in such a moment. What a crushing responsibility!

But as we can see from the text, Jehoshaphat *allowed his fear to trigger his faith.* Sometimes you'll hear people say that fear and faith can't coexist. I disagree! When you read through the Scriptures, you find example after example of people who were desperately afraid and troubled, going through trying, dreadful situations, and their fear drove them to trust God.

You and I belong on our knees before a great and merciful God, and if it takes fear to drive us there, then so be it!

The great key in all of life is to surrender to God.

The best and most appropriate thing you can ever do is turn to the Lord with all your heart. If it takes some set of overwhelming circumstances to push you into His arms, then count those circumstances as your friends.

I used to know an old fellow who liked to ask people, "How are you gettin' along?" And if they replied, "Not bad, under the circumstances," he would reply, "What in the world are you doing under there?"

I finally learned to say "fine" when he asked me that question, and I spoiled all his fun. He did have a point, though. God never intended for His kids to live under the pressure and fear and worry of life's situations. Jesus tells us, "In the world you will have tribulation; but be of good cheer, I have overcome the world" (John 16:33).

Surrendering is a good idea when you are facing dark and hopeless times. But always surrender to God, not to the circumstances.

There is a very big difference.

It's one thing to sigh and shrug your shoulders and say, "Well, there's nothing I can do," and it's another thing altogether to surrender your situation to the Lord who loves you. When you surrender your life and your circumstances to God, everything changes.

Yielding to His will and His plan is step number

one. Once that is done, you can begin to ask Him some questions as you pray. Perhaps you might say something like this: *"God, what do You see?"* In other words, "How does this situation look from Your vantage point? Please help me to find Your perspective on my situation."

The second question you might ask is, *"God, what are You going to do?"*

Third, you might ask, *"God, what should I be doing?"*

That's exactly the point where James chapter 1 comes into play. When you lack wisdom, the apostle tells us, ask of God. But that asking is in the context of serious and distressing trials.

> My brethren, count it all joy when you fall into various trials, knowing that the testing of your faith produces patience. But let patience have its perfect work, that you may be perfect and

---

PRINCIPLE #6:
Always surrender to God...
never to your circumstances.

51

complete, lacking nothing. If any of you lacks wisdom, let him ask of God, who gives to all liberally and without reproach, and it will be given to him. (James 1:2–5)

In other words, "God, I don't know what's going on here. I know what I *see,* but I want to look to You. So I'm asking You for wisdom to let me see these things as they truly are."

When I'm facing a trial or a difficult circumstance, I find that I need a refresher course on God. I need to remind myself about the parting of the Red Sea. I need to remember about the manna from heaven, how Jesus healed the blind man, and how He stilled the storm with a single word.

I give myself a quick refresher course on God and His blessings to me, and that helps me surrender to Him…not to my circumstances.

6

Waiting and Listening

Now all Judah, with their little ones, their wives, and their children, stood before the LORD. Then the Spirit of the LORD came upon Jahaziel the son of Zechariah, the son of Benaiah, the son of Jeiel, the son of Mattaniah, a Levite of the sons of Asaph, in the midst of the assembly. And he said, "Listen, all you of Judah and you inhabitants of Jerusalem, and you, King Jehoshaphat! Thus says the LORD to you: 'Do not be afraid nor dismayed because of this great multitude, for the battle is not yours, but God's.'"

2 CHRONICLES 20:13–15

What a picture! *All* Judah stood before the Lord: men and women, husbands and wives, sons and daughters, grandfathers and grandmothers, teenagers and toddlers, and babes in their mothers' arms. Their king had just finished humbling himself and pouring out his heart for his people. His last words had been, "We do not know what to do, but our eyes are upon You."

Then, with nothing left to say, the great assembly fell silent.

And waited.

And listened.

Then the Lord began to speak.

Jehoshaphat could have kept this prayer concern private—just between him and an inner circle of advisors. "After all," he might have reasoned, "we don't want panic in the streets." But he refused to do that. Instead, he assembled the whole nation for a mass prayer meeting. Every man, woman, and child in Judah had a stake in this issue, so their king gathered them all together before the feet of God.

There's something powerful about praying together in a great assembly. Anyone who knows our church in Beaverton will tell you that our Thursday night prayer meeting is the most significant service of the week. Sunday morning is wonderful, Sunday night is always joyous and encouraging, but Thursday night is where the action is. The building is filled with people kneeling before God and crying out to Him in prayer.

When I recently went through some especially intensive chemotherapy treatments, I ended up having a very bad reaction that put me in the hospital for ten days. It was a serious time, and the pain was greater than anything I've ever experienced in my life. I was given morphine to help alleviate the pain. For ten days, day and night, Joyce sat in a chair next to my bed, helping to administer the morphine every twenty minutes and praying without ceasing. She knew how vulnerable I was in that moment to any potential complications.

I learned later that the whole church family had gathered to pray for me. As with the crisis in Judah, *all* the people gathered. Since those days I've received piles of notes and cards from children who wrote, "Pastor, my mom and dad and I prayed for you every day."

And the Lord did a mighty work. I'm back doing what I love more than anything else in life...back in the pulpit, shepherding the flock I love.

All because God's people prayed.

In the midst of hopeless and impossible times, what is it that moves heaven on our behalf? It's people who pour out their request before Him, then listen for His answer.

I think of the prophet Habakkuk, who cried out to God and spread out his complaint and great burden at the feet of the Lord. Then, when he was done, he didn't budge from his place until he heard the Lord's answer.

> I will climb up into my watchtower now and wait to see what the LORD will say to me and how he will answer my complaint. (Habakkuk 2:1, NLT)

Is that what you do after you've prayed? Do you climb up into your watchtower and wait for the answer? Do you begin to anticipate God's reply and earnestly listen for what He has to say to you and how He will direct you? Or do you hasten off to your activities and plunge back into the world of noise and confusion and ten thousand distractions?

Do you really expect God to speak?

After Habakkuk purposed to wait, the very next verse says, "Then the LORD answered me and said..." (Habakkuk 2:2). Likewise, as Jehoshaphat and Judah

---

PRINCIPLE #7:
Listen for His voice...
before you leave the place of prayer.

---

waited on the Lord, He answered their prayer. The Bible says, "Then the Spirit of the LORD came upon Jahaziel…. And he said…" (2 Chronicles 20:14–15).

Satan hates it when we pray, and he hates it even more when we wait on the Lord for His direction and help and counsel. Why doesn't he want us to listen to God? Because he wants us to be separated from the Lord. He doesn't want us to connect with Him. He doesn't want us to see God as our Father, as our Provider, or as the All-Powerful One. Our enemy would rather keep us busy—even in the Lord's work, if need be—than see us quiet our souls to listen for God's voice.

It isn't easy taking time to listen. Most of us are wired for action, for doing. Standing and waiting, as Judah did on that historic day, is a challenge for us.

Susanna Wesley, mother to Charles and John Wesley, had seventeen children. Most of us can only imagine how hectic things became in that household. Just think of the incredible noise and confusion two or three kids can generate on a rainy day indoors. How would you like to try on seventeen for size? It would be like running a wild 'n' wooly day-care center single-handedly—only you never get to leave for the quiet of home at night because you *are* home.

One of the most difficult things for this godly

woman was finding a time and place to pray each day. Because there were so many children occupying every corner of the house, she had no place to go for a quiet moment, no place to retreat. That's when she came up with this radical solution. She told all the children that when they saw her sitting in the kitchen with her apron pulled up over her head, she was talking to God, and they weren't to disturb her.

That story makes me think of a more contemporary illustration. My friend Amos Dodge told me about his dear mom and her designated prayer place. There were "only" eleven children in the Dodge family, but they didn't have a house. They all lived in a thirty-five-foot travel trailer, which they pulled with one of those huge old Cadillac Fleetwoods.

When life became too hectic and the noise and confusion closed in on her, Mrs. Dodge would slip out to the Cadillac, sit in the backseat, bow her head, and pray. The kids, busy in their games and pursuits, would suddenly miss her and wonder where she'd gone.

Several of them would finally think to look outside, and sure enough, there she would be in the backseat, head bowed, talking to the Lord. Amos told me that the kids knew better than to bother her in that place of retreat. Everyone knew that was Mother's place to be quiet before God. If you didn't want to find yourself in serious trouble, you'd give that old Caddy a wide berth. And the God who sat in the driver's seat of this dear woman's life gave her many remarkable and amazing answers to prayer.

Just one more story. Dr. Eno, one of my professors in Bible college, told us about his morning prayer times when he was a young pastor at a tiny church in Canada. He was just starting in his ministry, and he was trying to adjust to the deep snow and below-zero temperatures.

His flock was small and conditions were harsh, but Dr. Eno was a very godly man who cared deeply about the small flock entrusted into his care. He would always get up at four o'clock in the morning to pray. The little house, of course, was freezing cold in those dark hours before dawn, and their only source of heat was the wood-burning cooking stove in the kitchen.

So Dr. Eno would start a fire in the stove, get down on his knees in that icy kitchen, and put his head into the oven so he could feel the warmth while he prayed. When he told the class that story, I remember how several of us ministry students laughed. It was such a ridiculous picture. A preacher with his head in the oven! Yet as the years have gone by, I don't laugh about that anymore. I know how desperately I need God's strength and wisdom in my life and ministry and how I need to make prayer a priority like Dr. Eno did.

He used to tell us, "You can do a whole lot of things to ready yourself for the ministry. You can read all the books and go to all the classes. But nothing will prepare you for challenging situations like being on your knees every morning of your life."

Now maybe you think it sounds kind of silly to pray with an apron over your face…or in the backseat of an old Cadillac…or with your head in the oven. And maybe it is. But where do *you* pray? How are you making prayer and listening to God a priority in *your* life?

7

Divine Reconnaissance

And he said, "Listen, all you of Judah and you inhabitants of Jerusalem, and you, King Jehoshaphat! Thus says the LORD to you: 'Do not be afraid nor dismayed because of this great multitude, for the battle is not yours, but God's. Tomorrow go down against them. They will surely come up by the Ascent of Ziz, and you will find them at the end of the brook before the Wilderness of Jeruel.'"

2 CHRONICLES 20:15–16

The Lord not only encouraged His people not to be afraid, He not only assured them of a great victory, but also reported to them precisely where the enemy was and what the enemy was planning to do.

"They will surely come up by the Ascent of Ziz."

The activities of the enemy are never a mystery to God. The counsels of hell are no more closed to Him than the counsels of men or angels. If you want to know anything about the enemy, don't go looking under rocks and in dark corners. Go to God. He's the One with the information you need.

These verses always remind me of an incident from a number of years ago. I was preaching at a little church somewhere in Central Oregon, and the good folks put me up at one of the only motels in town. The room was certainly nothing to write home about, but those sorts of things never matter much to me. All I wanted was to take a shower and hit the sack.

About two in the morning something aroused me from a deep sleep—a noise in my room.

I lay wide awake, holding my breath and listening. Was it a prowler? Would I have to defend myself? I knew one thing: If he grabbed my wallet, he was going to be sorely disappointed.

The more I listened, however, the more convinced I became that the intruder wasn't of the two-legged variety. And the noise I heard wasn't the sound of footsteps or someone groping through the room in the dark.

PRINCIPLE #8:
Ask God about Satan's plans…
before the enemy steals your most precious treasures.

It was the sound of chewing.

My uninvited guest was, no doubt, some kind of bewhiskered furry critter, and I strongly suspected a rat. *Oh terrific,* I thought. The worst part about it was that I knew exactly what he was dining on: my beloved bag of Snickers candy bars.

I lay there listening to my favorite snack being consumed. I could imagine him biting through the wrapper to get at the fresh milk chocolate, chewy caramel, crunchy peanuts, and creamy nougat.

What in the world am I going to do? I asked myself. Of course, the longer you lie there, the bigger the rat becomes. First he's the size of a normal rat, then he's as big as a Chihuahua, then he's a pit bull, swallowing whole Snickers bars at a single gulp. I could roll over and try to go back to sleep, but what would the rat do when he was finished with the candy? What if he fancied a bite or two of preacher for dessert?

I had to do something. Finally, I came up with a plan of reaching over to flip on the light and flinging my pillow at him in the same moment. I counted one, two, *three*—and flew into action. Untroubled by my mighty pillow toss, the rat left dining behind and scooted for the bathroom. *Now what?* Well, at least I had him cornered.

Or not.

He apparently maintained his own back door—a crack in the floor by the tub. I went back to bed with one thought uppermost in my mind. *He's coming back with his whole family.*

But he didn't come back. He'd already enjoyed a delightful midnight repast, and he probably slept as well as I did.

Sometime later, however, I found myself thinking about that rat chewing away at my Snickers while I was asleep and unaware. It's really a little parable of our lives—and what can happen if we don't seek the Lord's face and remain alert and diligent. Throughout my years of pastoral ministry, I've counseled with individuals and couples who have discovered to their dismay that precious things in their lives had been chewed away by the enemy while they were unaware. One day they looked up and suddenly realized that some of the things they loved most were gone.

If you're listening to God, as Jehoshaphat and the people of Judah did on that amazing day, He will show you where the enemy is approaching and how he plans to attack you. *"They will surely come up by the Ascent of Ziz, and you will find them at the end of the brook before the Wilderness of Jeruel"* (2 Chronicles 20:16)

Now that's better military intelligence than you could hope for with satellite photos and electronic listening devices. God didn't give Jehoshaphat several possible scenarios. He didn't reveal what the enemy might do or how they might advance; He told them what they *would* do, and precisely where they could be found.

That's the kind of information you get when you seek God's face every day, cry out to Him, listen to His voice, and obey Him. He will show you where the enemy is chewing away at your family, your marriage, your children, your business, or your walk with Christ. You'll get information about where to go, what to do, and how to pray...before it's too late.

David prayed, "Free me from the trap that is set for me, for you are my refuge" (Psalm 31:4, NIV).

Sadly, people often come to see me after the trap has been sprung, after the damage has been done, after the Snickers bars are gone. Broken and weeping, they will say, "My wife is leaving me," or "My husband is having an affair," or "My son is in deep trouble," or "My teenage daughter is pregnant!" And they are in shock. They're stunned and amazed that such a thing could happen, and they tell me how they never foresaw it.

But God knew about it all along. He knows the secret, furtive movements of the enemy. He knows the cracks where the enemy comes up out of the ground in

the night, and He knows where we're vulnerable to loss.
Listening to God is very, very important, because otherwise you're going to turn around someday and discover that what you love most is gone—consumed in the night while you were asleep and unaware.

In an earlier book, I told the story about being out of town, in a hotel far from home, and having a frightening dream about my oldest son, Ron Jr.—a young teenager at the time. In my dream, Ron had somehow become everything he never has been in real life. He was standing on a corner, under a streetlight, with what looked to be a gang of thugs—all of them smoking dope. He was cynical, rebellious, hateful. His face was as hard as stone and his eyes full of mockery. He laughed in my face when I tried to talk to him and reason with him. I was so troubled that I woke up weeping. I immediately got down on my knees beside my bed in that pitch-black hotel room and began to cry out to the Lord about my boy.

"Lord," I said, "this isn't my son. He's never been that way. He's never acted like that. He's never been hateful or rebellious to Joyce or me."

"No," the Lord seemed to whisper to my heart, "but he could become that way…unless you pray."

I spent a good part of that night on my knees, praying for God's grace and protection over Ron's life, praying for wisdom as a father to be the kind of dad Ron needed.

I spoke about this incident in one of my sermons, and after the message a couple confronted me—with a challenge in their eyes. They said, "Are you suggesting that if we don't pray for our kids, they could turn out to be dopers or rebels?" By the time we were through talking, I had the distinct idea that they really didn't want to feel any responsibility for the spiritual protection of their children. All I could do was repeat to them what the Lord had said to me. If they wanted to wash their hands of any responsibility, that was between them and the Lord. But I'll tell you this: When the Spirit of God warns me about something that's going on in the lives of my children, this dad is going straight to his knees, crying out to God.

I want to be on the alert for my family. I want to be on the alert for my marriage. You will never hear me say, "Well, this could never happen to me," or "This could never happen in my family." The truth is, if I'm not vigilant, if I'm not laying my life and my family before the Lord each day and listening for His voice, I'm as vulnerable as anyone else.

And so are you.

The rat in the motel that ate my Snickers never knew it, but he had just consumed his last meal. The motel manager trapped him the next day and sent him on to his reward. You see, that chocolate-loving rodent had revealed his modus operandi. He had exposed himself. And the next time he stuck his furry little head up through that hole by the bathtub, he was toast.

That's the way it is in spiritual warfare, too. If you find yourself going through a difficult time or if you're facing overwhelming circumstances or intense spiritual attack, you should be the most encouraged person in the world. Why? Because whenever Satan lifts his head, he is never more vulnerable.

If you don't believe that, ask Goliath. If that nine-foot Philistine had never challenged God and God's people, he might have ended his days in a retirement center, playing checkers and smelling the pansies. Instead, his severed head ended up as a trophy— gripped in the hands of a shepherd boy named David.

I've seen it again and again through my years in the front lines of ministry. Satan can work behind the scenes, causing all manner of troubles and consternation. But the minute he steps out and launches a major attack, he makes himself vulnerable. The prayers of God's people will send him to a major defeat.

Satan's strategy of quietly seducing Judah to idolatry and immorality had worked very well through the years. But when he sent a vast army to launch a surprise attack against Jehoshaphat and Jerusalem, when he attempted to wipe out Judah with one bold stroke, he overreached himself. He became vulnerable to the heartfelt cry of God's people, and his armies were utterly *smashed.*

Thank God when the big attacks come. Shout hallelujah! Your enemy has just made himself vulnerable, and God will bring victory in response to the earnest prayers of His people.

8

Obedience or Passivity?

So they rose early in the morning and went out into the Wilderness of Tekoa.

2 Chronicles 20:20

When Judah received the word from the prophet, the country held a massive worship and praise meeting. The king "bowed his head with his face to the ground," and the whole nation—small and great, young and old—began worshiping the Lord with all their might. Their worship leaders, the Levites and the Korahites "stood up to praise the Lord God of Israel with voices loud and high" (2 Chronicles 20:18–19).

Then, the next morning, in the cold light of dawn, they hit the highway heading south…straight into the face of a vast army, which was bent on delivering death and destruction.

It's one thing to be part of an emotional worship meeting where you find yourself caught up in the music, where the tears flow, and where everybody is lifting their hands in praise and shouting glory to the Almighty. It's pretty exciting being a part of something like that, and when you lay your head on the pillow at night, the music and joy keep on echoing in your heart.

But then comes morning.

The emotions aren't as high as you're sitting on the edge of the bed, trying to get your eyes to focus. And the commitments you made to the Lord don't seem nearly so fresh or so vital as they were in the heat of your holy passion the night before.

Think of the army of Judah that morning. They were on their way to face an enemy force bigger than they'd ever imagined. Yesterday's prayer meeting was just that: yesterday's prayer meeting. Where were the shouts and songs? Where were the emotions and tears?

PRINCIPLE #9:
RESOLVE TO DO WHAT THE LORD
HAS TOLD YOU TO DO...

As they silently strapped on their sandals and picked up their shields and weapons, all of that holy glow may have seemed like a long time ago and far away.

Perhaps the king sensed something like that, because he took time to remind them of a few things before they set off together:

> "Listen to me, all you people of Judah and Jerusalem! Believe in the LORD your God, and you will be able to stand firm. Believe in his prophets, and you will succeed." (2 Chronicles 20:20, NLT)

Why did the king find it necessary to remind his people to believe in the Lord and in His prophets? Could there have been some that morning who weren't standing firm? Were there some who had begun to doubt the prophet's bold words? Possibly there were. Even so, they got up early in the morning and set off anyway. They were obedient to the voice of the Lord.

It's a fact: God functions in the midst of obedience; Satan functions in the midst of passivity. If you want God to work in your life, just begin to *do* what He has said. Start the gears of your will in motion, whether your emotions are engaged or not.

Let's face it, there are a lot of us who are educated

way beyond our experience. We *know* a lot more than we *do.* I've observed a good many believers who know the Word, who understand God's promises, and who can quote Scripture until the cows come home. But it's really not doing them (or anybody else) much good until they begin to step out in faith and act on what they believe.

The Western church is overflowing with books, tapes, conferences, and seminars. More and more people are learning more and more principles. Sometimes people deceive themselves into thinking that the more they know, the more they've studied, the better they understand Greek and Hebrew, the more pleasing to God they will be. Not necessarily! All of that knowledge counts for nothing if it doesn't translate into action.

I firmly believe that when men and women step forward in faith and begin to do what they know and believe, they set the power of heaven in motion. God responds when He sees movement. God moves on behalf of doers.

Noah built an ark.

Abraham went to a land he'd never seen.

Joshua stepped into the Jordan at flood tide.

Mary told Gabriel, "Behold the maidservant of the Lord! Let it be to me according to your word" (Luke 1:38).

God is looking for people who not only hear what

He says, who not only memorize principles and attend seminars, but who will break the inertia, step out in faith, and begin to do what He commands.

Has the Lord spoken to you about showing more love toward your spouse? Then get up in the morning and start doing it whether you feel like it or not, whether he or she "merits" it or not.

Has the Lord spoken to you about talking to your neighbor concerning faith in Christ? You may never find that elusive "ideal moment." Just open your mouth and launch into it.

Has the Lord nudged you about tithing or giving a certain amount of money to some aspect of His work? Get up in the morning and write that check. Don't wait for the emotions or the organ music or the return of the "holy glow." Just be obedient to His voice, and watch Him begin to work in your life.

If you become passive, if you put obedience to the Lord on hold, if you decide to wait for a better or more inspiring day to do what the Lord has told you to do, then watch out! Satan will rob you right down to your underwear. One day you will wake up, look around you, and say, "What happened?" What happened to my faith? What happened to my marriage? What happened to my children? What happened to all of those things that were so precious to me?

Do you see the immediacy of what God's people did in this account? They got up early in the morning. Nobody slept in that day. Nobody stayed in the barracks polishing his armor. They stepped right into obedience, and as they did, the mighty power of God began to flow. Out ahead of them, in the camp of the enemy, despair and confusion began to descend as God's children moved in obedience.

That's why I think some people never get to experience the victory and blessing they really long for in their lives. It's because they don't follow through with what God has shown them to do. They hear God's voice, but then they rationalize it away and miss the opportunity for greatness in His kingdom.

My friend Steve Savelich has always reminded me that acts of obedience are always followed by great acts of God. He lets us do what we can do, and then He does what we could never do. For instance...

> You can build an ark, but only God
> can bring the great flood.
> You can march around the walls of
> Jericho, but only God can bring them
> down.

You can have people sit in groups of fifty, but only God can feed five thousand from a tiny sack lunch.

You can take steps of obedience in your marriage, but only God can bring the restoration and blessing.

Acts of obedience, doing what you know He wants you to do, are followed by acts of God. God's going to do something just as soon as you do.

9

Stand Still

"You will not need to fight in this battle.
Position yourselves, stand still and see the salvation
of the Lord, who is with you, O Judah and Jerusalem!"

2 Chronicles 20:17

When it came to being obedient, the army of Judah needed to stir themselves that morning and put themselves in position to see God work. But when it came to the actual battle, Judah didn't need to fire a single arrow or throw a single spear.

In fact, the Lord told them to position themselves and "stand still." Jehoshaphat and Judah had been obedient; now it was time for God to go into action.

I know that it sounds like a contradiction to the previous chapter, but you can't escape the biblical facts: There are some things about God you'll never see, you'll never experience, unless you stand still, cease all your efforts, and wait on Him to work.

"Be still, and know that I am God," the Lord tells us in Psalm 46:10.

"Stand still and see [My] salvation," the Lord tells us in 2 Chronicles 20:17.

Be still before God when you are in serious trouble. When the people of the infant nation of Israel found themselves backed into an impossible corner, with the Red Sea before them and the armies of Pharaoh thundering behind them, Moses told them, "Do not be afraid. Stand still, and see the salvation of the LORD, which He will accomplish for you today…. The LORD will fight for you, and you shall hold your peace" (Exodus 14:13–14).

Be still before God when your options have vanished and there seems to be nowhere to turn. When the next generation of Israelites approached the flood-stage Jordan River, seeking to cross into the Promised Land, God instructed the priests to walk straight toward the

PRINCIPLE #10:
Cease from your own striving…
and wait for Him to work.

water's edge and then said "ye shall stand still in Jordan" (Joshua 3:8, KJV). As the soles of their sandals touched the water, God stopped the flow of the river, allowing the waters to pile up in a heap upstream.

Many times in life, God will bring His people to the brink of impossibility, to the edge of an uncrossable precipice. And He says to us, "People of faith, stand still and watch Me do a work."

In your fear and anxiety, you may begin to say to yourself, "I'm doing what the Lord has told me to do, but I don't see anything happening." No, you may not see it—not right away at least. But God is doing something upstream. Even when you don't see the immediate evidence, God's working upstream and His work is coming your way.

How difficult standing still seems to us at times. There are seasons in our lives when we find ourselves facing circumstances that are deadly serious. We're not talking about something casual here. We're talking about a sick child…a failing marriage…a financial emergency. Think of the faith it takes to stand still. We're not *wired* to be still in the presence of crises! We're wired to do something, to start something, to plunge our hands into something, to fix it. We either want to run straight into the spears of the enemy and flail around ineffectually, or run away from the enemy in a blind panic.

But God has His own ways of compelling us to stand still, doesn't He? Remember what David wrote in the Shepherd's Psalm?

He makes me to lie down in green pastures;
He leads me beside the still waters.
(Psalm 23:2)

He *makes* me lie down? Yes, He will do that because I am a stubborn, foolish sheep sometimes, and I have no idea what to do or what is best for me. And because I can't find those green pastures or still waters by running blindly about the landscape, He puts some pressure on me and makes me slow down.

When I was little, I remember sitting by my mother in church and fiddling around and squirming during the message. Mom would say, "Be quiet now! Be still." And if I still kept fidgeting around and distracting people, she would reach over and grab my knee and start squeezing it. Where in the world did my sweet mother get those fingers of iron? And how could I be antsy and squirmy when my knee was being compressed to half its normal size?

From my own experience, I've found that God does the same thing sometimes. It isn't beyond Him to squeeze us a little, so that we will be still and experience His power and grace and provision in our lives.

I love what my friend Amos Dodge says: "While we're waiting, God is working."

The Music
of Obedience

And when he had consulted with the people,
he appointed those who should sing to the LORD, and who
should praise the beauty of holiness, as they went out
before the army and were saying:
"Praise the LORD,
For His mercy endures forever."

2 CHRONICLES 20:21

Whohen you face overwhelming odds, what do you say? His mercy endures! That's what the singers declared as they walked out ahead of the army into the teeth of the enemy position. No matter what—victory or defeat, sunlight or storm, health or illness, life or death—His mercies are going to last. As a prophet would declare years later,

> Through the LORD's mercies we are not con-
> sumed,
>> Because His compassions fail not.

They are new every morning;
  Great is Your faithfulness.
(Lamentations 3:22–23)

When Jehoshaphat leaned on the Lord's enduring mercy, it certainly wasn't a first-time experience. The Scriptures declare that our God has been merciful, is merciful, and will be merciful forever. Why could I not say that He will be merciful with me, right now, in whatever experience I happen to be facing?

When you face overwhelming odds, what do you say? *His mercy endures!*

When you face financial pressures, what do you say? *His mercy endures!*

When you face challenging health issues, what do you say? *His mercy endures!*

Mercy reminds us that God keeps on loving and giving and forgiving; He never runs out of grace. He never comes up short of compassion. You can't exhaust His love. Now I'm one of the nicest guys you'll ever meet, but after a while, you can exhaust my love and mercy. And I've got a hunch I could exhaust yours, too. There is a limit to our love and our mercy, but not to His.

God's character has to be the basis of our hope. He knows everything, and sees everything, and because

He's been faithful in the past, we know He is going to be faithful in the future. That principle resounds from beginning to end in this story. King Jehoshaphat rehearses God's character and moves forward in confidence and obedience.

Through many dark and difficult days in my own life, I've declared with David: "My times are in Your hand" (Psalm 31:15). And it's true. I can rest in the fact that all of my days and all of my hours rest in my Father's hands…and He is merciful. There have been times in the hospital when I knew great pain and overwhelming weakness, yet was comforted by the knowledge that He is in complete control of every detail, and that His mercy is great.

I wonder what it must have sounded like on that early morning in Judah when the choir marched in front of the army. I wonder what it sounded like from afar to the enemy. They would have heard something indistinguishable in the distance…something like a great wind, something like a storm, something like thunder. As the people of God drew nearer to the Ascent of Ziz, some among the Edomites might have imagined that the wind sounded like the voice of a great multitude, growing louder and louder.

Those who were in the vanguard of the enemy force may have begun to pick out words here and there. And how did those words sound to the ears of the adversary?

"Praise the LORD, for His mercy endures forever."

Did it puzzle them? Did it fill their hearts with wonder? Did it envelop them with a cold wave of dread? Did it begin to strip away their hope, their confidence, their boldness?

The people of Judah weren't running. They weren't attacking. They were just…standing there and…*singing.* How could it be? What did it mean?

To the people who marched and sang, I believe the message was this: God's mercy is going to endure in the midst of all this. God's mercy will outlast this attack. God will overcome this situation and bring us along!

When David says, "My times are in Your hands," I think he's basically saying, "Lord, You rule our life. Circumstances don't."

And that is what those people were saying down at the battle line. "Listen, Moabites and all you enemies of the living God! You don't control us! Circumstances don't rule our lives; *God* does. Our times are in His hands, and that is where we are resting."

It reminds me of what my wife said to me right after I got the diagnosis of leukemia. She put her arms around me and said, "The servant of the Lord is indestructible until God is finished with him."

And what happens when He *is* finished? Why, He takes us immediately into His presence where we'll be surrounded by joy and radiance and singing and inexpressible peace and life everlasting.

That's mercy! It will outlast everything you and I will ever face.

I've heard messages on this chapter of Scripture where the speaker begins with the end of the story: The song the choir sang as they led the army toward the enemy camp.

People will say, "Just begin singing a song of praise and God will do a work." Some people teach that a song is all it takes. Just sing and God will give you a miracle. Just shout praise in the face of your troubles and God will intervene.

These folks do have a point. Worship *is* powerful, and Scripture does speak of songs of deliverance. But if they think that it's a simple chorus that moved heaven or brought despair and destruction to the enemy, then they're mistaken. The people of Judah did sing of God's mercies on that glorious morning, but prior to that, they invited heaven's mighty intervention because of the way they and their king were living.

Jehoshaphat, remember, "did not seek the Baals,

but sought the God of his father, and walked in His commandments" (2 Chronicles 17:3–4).

Jehoshaphat "removed the wooden images from the land and...prepared [his] heart to seek God" (2 Chronicles 19:3).

Jehoshaphat "set himself to seek the LORD" when terrible trials entered his life (2 Chronicles 20:3).

Jehoshaphat recited God's résumé before the whole nation, declaring His deliverance, faithfulness, and power (2 Chronicles 20:6–11) .

Jehoshaphat freely admitted he had no strength or wisdom of his own; he was waiting on God alone for help and deliverance (2 Chronicles 20:12).

Jehoshaphat and all the people of Judah were faithful to do exactly as God commanded them, believing that His Word was truth, even if it disagreed with the "facts" (2 Chronicles 20:20).

Then they began to sing, *then* God began to deliver, and *then* they gathered up the spoils. It was more than the music of praise; it was the music of obedience. It was the music of lives lived in daily communion with Him.

God loves it when people worship without motives, clinging only to His Word and His promises. And that's why I love this part of the story. The people of Judah who marched toward a vast enemy army that morning could not see the future. The choir marching out in front of the troops sang God's praises even though they didn't know what would happen when they reached the Ascent of Ziz.

It's easy to worship *after* the battle has been won, *after* the spoils have been gathered. It's easy to praise God after you've received the answers to your prayers. But God's heart is moved when His people worship Him in faith, resting in His Word and His character alone.

I've seen lots of people praise God when the promotion comes…when the cancer tests come back normal…when the marriage is restored…when the unexpected check comes in the mail…when the loved one finally yields to Jesus Christ…when the runaway child returns home. But it's not as common to hear those same songs of praise from a throat constricted by weeping…when the promotion hasn't come…when the doctor's report isn't so good…when the marriage is still struggling…when the bill collectors are knocking on the door…when the child has been gone a long time, and there is no word.

The book of Hebrews calls that "a sacrifice of praise," and the aroma that rises from such an offering is very, very fragrant in the courts of heaven.

Remember Paul and Silas, deep in the bowels of

that Philippian prison? It was midnight dark. Their feet were in stocks. Their backs were deeply bruised and running with blood from a severe beating. Their ministry was at a standstill. They had no idea when or even if they would be released.

And what does the Scripture say? "At midnight Paul and Silas were praying and singing hymns to God" (Acts 16:25).

Something happened that night. The earth shook. Chains shattered. Prison doors swung open. Prisoners walked free.

You might say that the prayer of faith moved heaven.

And you would be right.

Multnomah Publishers®

The publisher and author would love to hear your comments about this book. *Please contact us at:*
www.multnomah.net/ronmehl

WHAT GOD WHISPERS IN THE NIGHT

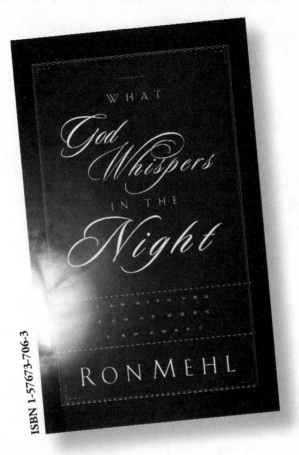

ISBN 1-57673-706-3

In this expanded, revised hardback edition of *The Cure for a Troubled Heart*, Ron Mehl has crafted a book of tender encouragement for Christians dealing with seasons of difficulty. Mehl points out that in moments of struggle and heartache, human coping strategies can offer only temporary and superficial help. He highlights key Scriptures which give powerful direction and comfort—empowering the struggling believer through God's whispered messages: "I Am Awake," "I Am at Work," and "I Am on Watch." With moving, contemporary illustrations, meaty content, and a dynamic epilogue, Mehl skillfully unveils the ways the Lord's love can penetrate pain and restore hope and peace in any circumstance.

GOD WORKS THE NIGHT SHIFT

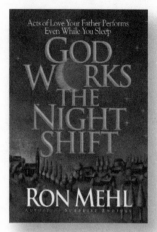

ISBN 0-88070-718-6 PA
ISBN 0-88070-654-6 HD

Sometimes we feel that God is moving by leaps and bounds in the lives of others, but not in our own life. When we are going through difficult times it may seem as though other people have been richly blessed—while our own life is completely empty. Pastor Ron Mehl assures readers that, despite the way things sometimes appear, God is continually at work in our life and often does His best work in the darkness. As men and women take a closer look at the God who "works the night shift," they will learn about the unceasing acts of love He performs for them even while they sleep.

SURPRISE ENDINGS

For all of the readers who have ever wondered whether God sees their suffering...for those who wonder if there is any purpose to their pain...for those who wonder why God allows their struggles to continue... Ron Mehl shines new light on life's bad things, revealing their part in God's plan to shower us with His love.

ISBN 0-88070-828-X PA